ADAM ZAGAJEWSKI

Eternal Enemies

TRANSLATED BY CLARE CAVANAGH

ADAM ZAGAJEWSKI was born in Lvov, Poland, in 1945. His previous books include *Tremor, Canvas, Two Cities, Mysticism for Beginners, Another Beauty, Without End,* and *A Defense of Ardor*—all published by FSG. He lives in Kraków, Paris, and Chicago.

CLARE CAVANAGH is a professor of Slavic languages and literatures at Northwestern University. She has translated numerous volumes of Polish poetry and prose, including the work of Wisława Szymborska, and is working on a biography of Czesław Miłosz, to be published by FSG.

POETRY

Tremor: Selected Poems

Canvas

Mysticism for Beginners

Without End: New and Selected Poems

ESSAYS

Solidarity, Solitude

Two Cities

Another Beauty

A Defense of Ardor

Eternal Enemies

FARRAR, STRAUS AND GIROUX NEW YORK

TRANSLATED FROM THE POLISH BY CLARE CAVANAGH

Eternal Enemies
Adam Zagajewski

FARRAR, STRAUS AND GIROUX
18 West 18th Street, New York 10011

Printed in the United States of America
Published in 2008 by Farrar, Straus and Giroux
First paperback edition, 2009

Some of these poems originally appeared, in different form,
in *Five Points*, *The New Republic*, *The New York Review
of Books*, *The New Yorker*, *Ploughshares*, and *Poetry*.

The Library of Congress has cataloged the hardcover edition as follows:
Zagajewski, Adam, 1945–
    [Poems. English. Selections]
    Eternal enemies / Adam Zagajewski ; translated from the Polish
by Clare Cavanagh.— 1st ed.
        p.   cm.
    ISBN-13: 978-0-374-21634-4 (alk. paper)
    ISBN-10: 0-374-21634-7 (alk. paper)
    1. Zagajewski, Adam, 1945– —Translations into English.
I. Cavanagh, Clare.   II. Title.

PG7185.A32 A2 2008
891.8'5173—dc22

                                        2007042855

Paperback ISBN-13: 978-0-374-53160-7
Paperback ISBN-10: 0-374-53160-9

Designed by Quemadura

www.fsgbooks.com

P1

TO MAYA, *toujours*

I

II

III

I

STAR

I returned to you years later,
gray and lovely city,
unchanging city
buried in the waters of the past.

I'm no longer the student
of philosophy, poetry, and curiosity,
I'm not the young poet who wrote
too many lines

and wandered in the maze
of narrow streets and illusions.
The sovereign of clocks and shadows
has touched my brow with his hand,

but still I'm guided by
a star by brightness
and only brightness
can undo or save me.

EN ROUTE

1. WITHOUT BAGGAGE

To travel without baggage, sleep in the train
on a hard wooden bench,
forget your native land,
emerge from small stations
when a gray sky rises
and fishing boats head to sea.

2. IN BELGIUM

It was drizzling in Belgium
and the river wound between hills.
I thought, I'm so imperfect.
The trees sat in the meadows
like priests in green cassocks.
October was hiding in the weeds.
No, ma'am, I said,
this is the nontalking compartment.

3. A HAWK CIRCLES ABOVE THE HIGHWAY

It will be disappointed if it swoops down
on sheet iron, on gas,
on a tape of tawdry music,
on our narrow hearts.

4. MONT BLANC

It shines from afar, white and cautious,
like a lantern for shadows.

5. SEGESTA

On the meadow a vast temple —
a wild animal
open to the sky.

6. SUMMER

Summer was gigantic, triumphant —
and our little car looked lost
on the road going to Verdun.

7. THE STATION IN BYTOM

In the underground tunnel
cigarette butts grow,
not daisies.
It stinks of loneliness.

8. RETIRED PEOPLE ON A FIELD TRIP

They're learning to walk
on land.

9. GULLS

Eternity doesn't travel,
eternity waits.
In a fishing port
only the gulls are chatty.

10. THE THEATER IN TAORMINA

From the theater in Taormina you spot
the snow on Etna's peak
and the gleaming sea.
Which is the better actor?

11. A BLACK CAT

A black cat comes out to greet us
as if to say, look at me
and not some old Romanesque church.
I'm alive.

12. A ROMANESQUE CHURCH

At the bottom of the valley
a Romanesque church at rest:
there's wine in this cask.

13. LIGHT

Light on the walls of old houses,
June.
Passerby, open your eyes.

14. AT DAWN

The world's materiality at dawn—
and the soul's frailty.

MUSIC IN THE CAR

Music heard with you
at home or in the car
or even while strolling
didn't always sound as pristine
as piano tuners might wish—
it was sometimes mixed with voices
full of fear and pain,
and then that music
was more than music,
it was our living
and our dying.

THE SWALLOWS OF AUSCHWITZ

In the barracks' quiet,
in the silence of a summer Sunday,
the swallows' shrill cry.

Is this really all that's left
of human speech?

STOLARSKA STREET

The small crowd by the American consulate
ripples like a jellyfish in water.
A young Dominican strides down the sidewalk
and passersby yield piously.
I'm at home again, silent as a Buddhist.
I count the days of happiness and fretting,
days spent seeking you frantically,
finding just a metaphor, an image,
days of Ecclesiastes and the Psalmist.

I remember the heatstruck scent of heather,
the smell of sap in the forest by the sea,
the dark of a white chapel in Provence,
where only a candle's sun glowed.
I remember Greece's small olives,
Westphalia's gleaming railroads,
and the long trip to bid my mother goodbye
on an airplane where they showed a comedy,
everyone laughed loudly.

I returned to the city of sweet cakes,
bitter chocolate, and lovely funerals
(a grain of hope was once buried here),
the city of starched memory—
but the anxiety that drives wanderers,

and turns the wheels of bicycles, mills, and clocks,
won't leave me, it remains concealed
in my heart like a starving deserter
in an abandoned circus wagon.

GENEALOGY

I'll never know them,
those outmoded figures
—the same as we are,
yet completely different.
My imagination works to unlock
the mystery of their being,
it can't wait for the release
of memory's secret archives.

I see them in cramped classrooms,
in the small provincial towns
of the Hapsburgs' unhappy empire.
Poplars twitch hysterically
outside the windows
while snow and rain dictate
their own orthography.

They grip a useless scrap of chalk
helplessly in their fists,
in fingers black with ink.
They labor to reveal the world's mystery
to noisy, hungry children,
who only grow and scream.

My schoolmaster forebears fought
to calm an angry ocean
just like that mad artist
who rose above the waves
clutching his frail conductor's wand.

I imagine the void
of their exhaustion, empty moments
through which I spy
their life's core.

And I think that when I too
do my teaching,
they gaze in turn at me,

revising my mutterings,
correcting my mistakes

with the calm assurance of the dead.

KARMELICKA STREET

TO FRITZ STERN

Karmelicka Street, a sky blue tram, the sun,
September, the first day after vacation,
some have come home from long trips,
armored divisions enter Poland,
children off to school dressed in their best,
white and navy blue, like sails and sea,
like memory and grapes and inspiration.
The trees stand at attention, honoring
the power of young minds that haven't yet
known fire and sleep and can do what they want,
nothing can stop them
(not counting invisible limits).

The trees greet the young respectfully,
but you—be truthful—envy
that starting out, that setting off
from home, from childhood, from the sweet darkness
that tastes of almonds, raisins, and poppy seeds,
you stop by the store for bread
and then walk home, unhurried,
whistling and humming carelessly;
your school still hasn't started,
the teachers have gone, the masters remain,
distant as summer, your sleep sails through the clouds
across the sky.

LONG STREET

Thankless street—little dry goods stores
like sentries in Napoleon's frozen army;
country people peer into shop windows and their reflections
gaze back at dusty cars;
Long Street trudging slowly to the suburbs,
while the suburbs press toward the center.
Lumbering trams groove the street,
scentless perfume shops furrow it,
and after rainstorms mud instead of manna;
a street of dwarves and giants, creaking bikes,
a street of small towns clustered
in one room, napping after lunch,
heads dropped on a soiled tablecloth,
and clerics tangled in long cassocks;
unsightly street—coal rises here in fall,
and in August the boredom of white heat.

This is where you spent your first years
in the proud Renaissance town,
you dashed to lectures and military drills
in an outsized overcoat—
and now you wonder, can
you return to the rapture
of those years, can you still
know so little and want so much,

and wait, and go to sleep so swiftly,
and wake adroitly
so as not to startle your last dream
despite the December dawn's darkness.

Street long as patience.
Street long as flight from a fire,
as a dream that never
ends.

TADEUSZ KANTOR

He dressed in black,
like a clerk at an insurance bureau
who specializes in lost causes.
I'd spot him on Urzednicza
rushing for a streetcar,
and at Krzysztofory as he solemnly discharged
his duties, receiving other artists dressed in black.
I dismissed him with the pride
of someone who's done nothing himself
and despises the flaws of finished things.
Much later, though,
I saw *The Dead Class* and other plays,
and fell silent with fear and admiration—
I witnessed systematic dying,
decline, I saw how time
works on us, time stitched into clothes or rags,
into the face's slipping features, I saw
the work of tears and laughter, the gnashing of teeth,
I saw boredom and yearning at work, and how
prayer might live in us, if we would let it,
what blowhard military marches really are,
what killing is, and smiling,
and what wars are, seen or unseen, just or not,
what it means to be a Jew, a German, or
a Pole, or maybe just human,

why the elderly are childish,
and children dwell in aging bodies
on a high floor with no elevator and try
to tell us something, let us know, but it's useless,
in vain they wave gray handkerchiefs
stretching from their school desks scratched with penknives
—they already know that they have only
the countless ways of letting go,
the pathos of helpless smiles,
the innumerable ways of taking leave,
and they don't even hear the dirty stage sets
singing with them, singing shyly
and perhaps ascending into heaven.

THE POWER CINEMA

FOR BARBARA AND WOJCIECH PSZONIAK

Some Sundays were white
like sand on Baltic beaches.
In the morning footsteps sounded
from infrequent passersby.
The leaves of our trees kept watchful silence.
A fat priest prayed for everyone
who couldn't come to church.
Movie projectors gave intoxicating hiccups
as dust wandered crosswise through the light.
Meanwhile a skinny priest bewailed the times
and called us to strict mystic contemplation.
A few ladies grew slightly faint.
The screen in the Power Cinema was happy to receive
every film and every image—
the Indians felt right at home,
but Soviet heroes
were no less welcome.
After each showing a silence fell,
so deep that the police got nervous.
But in the afternoon the city slept,
mouth open, like an infant in a stroller.
Sometimes a wind stirred in the evening
and at dusk a storm would flicker

with an eerie, violet glow.
At midnight the frail moon
came back to a scrubbed sky.
On some Sundays it seemed
that God was close.

THE CHURCH OF CORPUS CHRISTI

We're next to the Jewish Quarter,
where mindful prayers rose
in another tongue, the speech of David,
which is like a nut, a cluster of grapes.

This church isn't lovely,
but it doesn't lack solemnity;
a set of vertical lines
and dust trembling in a sunbeam,

a shrine of minor revelations
and strenuous silence,
the terrain of longing
for those who have gone.

I don't know if I'll be admitted,
if my imperfect prayer
will enter the dark, trembling air,

if my endless questing
will halt within this church,
still and sated as a beehive.

WAS IT

Was it worth waiting in consulates
for some clerk's fleeting good humor
and waiting at the station for a late train,
seeing Etna in its Japanese cloak
and Paris at dawn, as Haussmann's conventional caryatids
came looming from the dark,
entering cheap restaurants
to the triumphal scent of garlic,
was it worth taking the underground
beneath I can't recall what city
to see the shades of not my ancestors,
flying in a tiny plane over an earthquake
in Seattle like a dragonfly above a fire, but also
scarcely breathing for three months, asking anxious questions,
forgetting the mysterious ways of grace,
reading in papers about betrayal, murder,
was it worth thinking, remembering, falling
into deepest sleep, where gray hallways
stretched, buying black books,
jotting only separate images
from a kaleidoscope more glorious than the cathedral
in Seville, which I haven't seen,
was it worth coming and going, was it—
yes no yes no
erase nothing.

RAINBOW

I returned to Long Street with its dark
halo of ancient grime—and to Karmelicka Street,
where drunks with blue faces await
the world's end in delirium tremens
like the anchorites of Antioch, and where
electric trams tremble from excess time,
to my youth, which didn't want
to wait and passed on, perished from long
fasting and strict vigils, I returned to
black side streets and used bookshops,
to conspiracies concealing
affection and treachery, to laziness,
to books, to boredom, to oblivion, to tea,
to death, which took so many
and gave no one back,
to Kazimierz, vacant district,
empty even of lamentation,
to a city of rain, rats, and garbage,
to childhood, which evaporated
like a puddle gleaming with a rainbow of gasoline,
to the university, still trying clumsily
to seduce yet another naive generation,
to a city now selling
even its own walls, since it sold
its fidelity and honor long ago, to a city

I love mistrustfully
and can offer nothing
except what I've forgotten and remember
except a poem, except life.

FRIENDS

My friends wait for me,
ironic, smiling sadly.

Where are the transparent palaces
we meant to build—

their lips say,
their aging lips.

Don't worry, friends,
those splendid kites

still soar in the autumn air,
still take us

to the place where harvests begin,
to bright days—

the place where scarred eyes
open.

SICILY

You led me across the vast meadow,
the three-cornered Common that is Sicily
for this town that doesn't know the sea,
you led me to the Syracuse
of cold kisses and we passed
through the endless ocean of the grass
like conquerors with clear consciences
(since we vanquished only ourselves),
in the evening, under a vast sky,
under sharp stars,
a sky spreading righteously
over what lasts
and the lazy river of remembrance.

DESCRIBING PAINTINGS

TO DANIEL STERN

We usually catch only a few details —
grapes from the seventeenth century,
still fresh and gleaming,
perhaps a fine ivory fork,
or a cross's wood and drops of blood,
and great suffering that has already dried.
The shiny parquet creaks.
We're in a strange town —
almost always in a strange town.
Somewhere a guard stands and yawns.
An ash branch sways outside the window.
It's absorbing,
describing static paintings.
Scholars devote tomes to it.
But we're alive,
full of memory and thought,
love, sometimes regret,
and at moments we take a special pride
because the future cries in us
and its tumult makes us human.

BLIZZARD

We were listening to music—
a little Bach, a little mournful Schubert.
For a moment we listened to the silence.
A blizzard roared outside,
the wind pressed its blue face
to the wall.
The dead raced past on sleds,
tossing snowballs
at our windows.

POETRY SEARCHES FOR RADIANCE

Poetry searches for radiance,
poetry is the kingly road
that leads us farthest.
We seek radiance in a gray hour,
at noon or in the chimneys of the dawn,
even on a bus, in November,
while an old priest nods beside us.

The waiter in a Chinese restaurant bursts into tears
and no one can think why.
Who knows, this may also be a quest,
like that moment at the seashore,
when a predatory ship appeared on the horizon
and stopped short, held still for a long while.
And also moments of deep joy

and countless moments of anxiety.
Let me see, I ask.
Let me persist, I say.
A cold rain falls at night.
In the streets and avenues of my city
quiet darkness is hard at work.
Poetry searches for radiance.

II

THE DICTION TEACHER RETIRES FROM THE THEATER SCHOOL

Tall, shy, dignified
in an old-fashioned way,

She bids farewell to students, faculty,
and looks around suspiciously.

She's sure they'll mangle their mother tongue
ruthlessly and go unpunished.

She takes the certificate (she'll check
for errors later). She turns and vanishes offstage,

in the spotlights' velvet shadows,
in silence.

We're left alone
to twist our tongues and lips.

IN A LITTLE APARTMENT

I ASK MY FATHER, "WHAT DO YOU
DO ALL DAY?" "I REMEMBER."

So in that dusty little apartment in Gliwice,
in a low block in the Soviet style
that says all towns should look like barracks,
and cramped rooms will defeat conspiracies,
where an old-fashioned wall clock marches on, unwearied,

he relives daily the mild September of '39, its whistling bombs,
and the Jesuit Garden in Lvov, gleaming
with the green glow of maples and ash trees and small birds,
kayaks on the Dniester, the scent of wicker and wet sand,
that hot day when you met a girl who studied law,

the trip by freight car to the west, the final border,
two hundred roses from the students
grateful for your help in '68,
and other episodes I'll never know,
the kiss of a girl who didn't become my mother,

the fear and sweet gooseberries of childhood, images drawn
from that calm abyss before I was.
Your memory works in the quiet apartment—in silence,
systematically, you struggle to retrieve for an instant
your painful century.

[34]

THE ORTHODOX LITURGY

Deep voices beg insistently for mercy
and have no self-defense
beyond their own glorious singing—though no one
is here, just a disc spinning
swiftly and invisibly.

One soloist recalls the voice
of Joseph Brodsky reciting his poems
before Americans, unconvinced
by any sort of resurrection,
but glad that somebody believed.

It's enough—or so we think—
that someone believes for us.

Low voices still sing.
Have mercy on us.

Have mercy on me too,
unseen Lord.

ROME, OPEN CITY

A March day, the trees are still naked, plane trees patiently
    await the leaves' green heat,
churches caked in dust, vermilion, ocher, sienna, and bordeaux,
    broad stains of cinnamon.
Why did we stop talking?
In the Barberini Palace fair Narcissus gazes at his own face,
    lifeless.
Brown city ceaselessly repeating: *mi dispiace.*
Brown city, entered by weary Greek gods
    like office workers from the provinces.
Today I want to see your eyes without anger.
    Brown city, growing on the hills.
Poems are short tragedies, portable, like transistor radios.
    Paul lies on the ground, it's night, a torch, the smell of pitch.
Impatient glances in cafés, someone yells, a small heap of coins
    lies on the table.
Why? Why not?
The roar of cars and scooters, hubbub of events.
    Poetry often vanishes, leaving only matchsticks.
Children run above the Tiber in funny school cloaks
    from the century's beginning:
nearby, cameras and spotlights. They're running for a film, not for you.
    David is ashamed of murdering Goliath.
Forgive my silence. Forgive your silence.
    City full of statues; only the fountains sing.

The holidays approach, when the heathens go to church.
    Via Giulia: magnolia blossoms keep their secret.
A moment of light costs just five hundred lire, which you toss
    into a black box.
We can meet on the Piazza Navona, if you want.
Matthew keeps asking himself: was I truly
    summoned to become human?

THE SEA

Shimmering among boulders, deep blue at noon,
ominous when summoned by the west wind,
but calm at night, inclined to make amends.

Tireless in small bays, commanding
countless hosts of crabs who march sideways
like damp veterans of the Punic Wars.

At midnight cutters sail from port: the glare
of a single light slices the darkness,
engines quake.

At the beach near Cefalù, on Sicily, we saw
countless heaps of trash, boxes, condoms,
cartons, a faded sign saying ANTONIO.

In love with the earth, always drawn to shore,
sending wave after wave—and each dies
exhausted, like a Greek messenger.

At dawn only whispers reach us,
the low murmur of pebbles cast on sand
(sensed even in the fishing town's small square).

The Mediterranean, where gods swam,
and the frigid Baltic, which I entered,
a skinny, trembling, twenty-year-old eel.

In love with the earth, thrusting into its cities, Stockholm,
Venice, listening to tourists laugh and chatter
before returning to its dark, unmoving source.

Your Atlantic, busy building up white dunes,
and the shy Pacific hiding in the deeps.

Light-winged gulls.
The last sailing ships, white canvas
billowing on crosses.

Slim canoes are manned by watchful hunters,
the sun rises in great silence.

Gray Baltic,
Arctic Ocean, mute,
the Ionian, world's origin and end.

READING MILOSZ

I read your poetry once more,
poems written by a rich man, knowing all,
and by a beggar, homeless,
an emigrant, alone.

You always wanted to go
beyond poetry, above it, soaring,
but also lower, to where our region
begins, modest and timid.

Sometimes your tone
transforms us for a moment,
we believe—truly—
that every day is sacred,

that poetry—how to put it?—
makes life rounder,
fuller, prouder, unashamed
of perfect formulation.

But evening arrives,
I lay my book aside,
and the city's ordinary din resumes—
somebody coughs, someone cries and curses.

WALK THROUGH THIS TOWN

Walk through this town at a gray hour
when sorrow hides in shady gates
and children play with great balls
that float like kites above
the poisoned wells of courtyards,
and, quiet, doubting, the last blackbird sings.

Think about your life which goes on,
though it's already lasted so long.

Could you voice the smallest fragment of the whole.

Could you name baseness when you saw it.

If you met someone truly living
would you know it?

Did you abuse high words?

Whom should you have been, who knows.
You love silence, and you've mastered
only silence, listening to words, music, and quiet:
why did you begin to speak, who knows.

Why in this age, why in a country
that wasn't born yet, who knows.
Why among exiles, in a flat that had been
German, amid grief and mourning
and vain hopes of a regained myth.

Why a childhood shadowed
by mining towers and not a forest's dark,
near a stream where a quiet dragonfly keeps watch
over the world's secret wholeness

—who knows.

And your love, which you lost and found,
and your God, who won't help those
who seek him,
and hides among theologians
with degrees.

Why just this town at a gray hour,
this dry tongue, these numb lips,
and so many questions before you leave
and go home to the kingdom
from which silence, rapture, and the wind
once came.

ORDINARY LIFE

TO CLARE CAVANAGH

Our life is ordinary,
I read in a crumpled paper
abandoned on a bench.
Our life is ordinary,
the philosophers told me.

Ordinary life, ordinary days and cares,
a concert, a conversation,
strolls on the town's outskirts,
good news, bad—

but objects and thoughts
were unfinished somehow,
rough drafts.

Houses and trees
desired something more
and in summer green meadows
covered the volcanic planet
like an overcoat tossed upon the ocean.

Black cinemas crave light.
Forests breathe feverishly,
clouds sing softly,
a golden oriole prays for rain.
Ordinary life desires.

MUSIC HEARD WITH YOU

MUSIC I HEARD WITH YOU WAS MORE
THAN MUSIC . . . — CONRAD AIKEN

Music heard with you
will stay with us always.

Grave Brahms and elegiac Schubert,
a few songs, Chopin's fourth ballad,

a few quartets with heart-
breaking chords (Beethoven, adagia),

the sadness of Shostakovich, who
didn't want to die.

The great choruses of Bach's Passions,
as if someone had summoned us,

demanding joy,
pure and impartial,

joy in which faith
is self-evident.

Some scraps of Lutoslawski
as fleeting as our thoughts.

A black woman singing blues
ran through us like shining steel,

though it reached us on the street
of an ugly, dirty town.

Mahler's endless marches,
the trumpet's voice that opens the Fifth Symphony

and the first part of the Ninth
(you sometimes call him "malheur!").

Mozart's despair in the Requiem,
his buoyant piano concertos—

you hummed them better than I did,
but we both know that.

Music heard with you
will grow still with us.

AT THE CATHEDRAL'S FOOT

In June once, in the evening,
returning from a long trip,
with memories of France's blooming trees
still fresh in our minds,
its yellow fields, green plane trees
sprinting before the car,

we sat on the curb at the cathedral's foot
and spoke softly about disasters,
about what lay ahead, the coming fear,
and someone said this was the best
we could do now —
to talk of darkness in that bright shadow.

IMPOSSIBLE FRIENDSHIPS

For example, with someone who no longer is,
who exists only in yellowed letters.

Or long walks beside a stream,
whose depths hold hidden

porcelain cups—and the talks about philosophy
with a timid student or the postman.

A passerby with proud eyes
whom you'll never know.

Friendship with this world, ever more perfect
(if not for the salty smell of blood).

The old man sipping coffee
in St.-Lazare, who reminds you of someone.

Faces flashing by
in local trains—

the happy faces of travelers headed perhaps
for a splendid ball, or a beheading.

And friendship with yourself
—since after all you don't know who you are.

[47]

RAIN DROP

In the drop of rain that stopped
outside my window, dawdling,
an oval, shining shape appears
and I see Mrs. Czolga again,
stuffing a statuesque goose in her kitchen.
Carts, dark and chthonic, carried coal,
rolling over wooden cobbles,
asking—do you want to live?
But after the great war of death
we wanted life so much.
A red-hot iron pressed the past,
at dawn German blackbirds
sang the poems of Georg Trakl,
and we wanted life and dreams.

BUTTERFLIES

It's a December night, the century's end, dark and calm,
   draws near.
I slowly read friends' poems, look at photographs,
   the spines of books.
Where has C. gone? What's become of bumptious K. and smiling T. ?
   What ever happened to B. and N. ?
Some have been dead a millennium, while others, debutants, died
   just the other month.
Are they together? In a desert with a crimson dawn?
   We don't know where they live.
By a mountain stream where butterflies play?
   In a town scented with mignonette?
Die Toten reiten schnell, S. repeated eagerly (he too
   is gone).
They ride little horses in the steppe's quiet, beneath a round yellow
   cloud.
Maybe they steal coal at a little railroad stop in Asia and melt
   snow in sooty pots
like those transported in freight cars.
   (Do they have camps and barbed wire?)
Do they play checkers? Listen to music? Do they see Christ?
   They dictate poems to the living.
They paint bison on cave walls, begin building
   the cathedral in Beauvais.

Have they grasped the sense of evil, which eludes us,
   and forgiven those who persecuted them?
They wade through an arctic glacier, soft from the August heat.
   Do they weep? Regret?
Talk on telephones for hours? Hold their tongues? Are they here among us?
   Nowhere?
I read poems, listen to the mighty whisper
   of night and blood.

IN A STRANGE CITY

The faint, almost fantastic
scent of the Mediterranean,
crowds on streets at midnight,
a festival begins,
we don't know which.
A scrawny cat slips
past our knees,
gypsies eat supper
as if singing;
white houses beyond them,
an unknown tongue.
Happiness.

CAMOGLI

High old houses above the water
and a drowsy cat waiting for fishermen
on furled white nets:
a quiet November in Camogli—
pensioners sunbathe on lounge chairs,
the sun rotates sluggishly
and stones revolve slowly
on the gravelly shore,
but it, the sea, keeps turning landward,
wave after wave, as if wondering
what happened to summer's plans
and our dreams,
what has our youth become.

BOGLIASCO: THE CHURCH SQUARE

A photographer develops film,
the sexton scrutinizes
walls and trees,
boys play ball,
a dry cleaner purges the conscience
of this quiet town,
three elderly ladies discuss the world's end—
but evening brings back
the sea's tumult
and its din
returns the day just past
into oblivion.

STAGLIENO

Don't linger in the graveyard
where the nineteenth century, dusty, charmless,
still repents; you'll be received
by doctors in stucco frock coats
buttoned to the throat, in stone cravats,
stone barristers with stony, slightly mournful
smiles (duplicity has outlived itself).
You'll be received by patresfamilias, professors
and children, marble children, plaster dogs,
always flawlessly obedient.
You'll see the past, meet
your older brothers, glimpse
Pompeii, submerged
in time's gray lava.

TWO-HEADED BOY

The fifteen-year-old boy carried a kitten
inside his dark blue windbreaker.
Its tiny head turned,
its large eyes watching
everything more cautiously
than human eyes.

Safe in the warm train,
I compare the boy's lazy stare
to the kitten's pupils,
alert and narrow.

The two-headed boy sitting across from me
made richer by an animal's unrest.

OUR WORLD

IN MEMORIAM W. G. SEBALD

I never met him, I only knew
his books and the odd photos, as if
purchased in a secondhand shop, and human
fates discovered secondhand,
and a voice quietly narrating,
a gaze that caught so much,
a gaze turned back,
avoiding neither fear
nor rapture;
        and our world in his prose,
our world, so calm—but
full of crimes perfectly forgotten,
even in lovely towns
on the coast of one sea or another,
our world full of empty churches,
rutted with railroad tracks, scars
of ancient trenches, highways,
cleft by uncertainty, our blind world
smaller now by you.

SMALL OBJECTS

My contemporaries like small objects,
dried starfish that have forgotten the sea,
melancholy stopped clocks, postcards
sent from vanished cities,
and blackened with illegible script,
in which they discern words
like "yearning," "illness," or "the end."
They marvel at dormant volcanoes.
They don't desire light.

.

DEFENDING POETRY, ETC.

Yes, defending poetry, high style, etc.,
but also summer evenings in a small town,
where gardens waft and cats sit quietly
on doorsteps, like Chinese philosophers.

SUBJECT: BRODSKY

Please note: born in May,
in a damp city (hence the motif: water),
soon to be surrounded by an army
whose officers kept Hölderlin
in their backpacks, but, alas, they had
no time for reading. Too much to do.

Tone—sardonic, despair—authentic.
Always en route, from Mexico to Venice,
lover and crusader, who campaigned
ceaselessly for his unlikely party
(name: Poetry versus the Infinite,
or PVI, if you prefer abbreviations).

In every city and in every port
he had his agents; he sometimes sang his poems
before an avid crowd that didn't catch
a word. Afterwards, exhausted, he'd smoke a Gauloise
on a cement embankment, gulls circling overhead,
as if above the Baltic, back home.

Vast intelligence. Favorite topic: time
versus thought, which chases phantoms,
revives Mary Stuart, Daedalus, Tiberius.
Poetry should be like horse racing;

wild horses, with jockeys made of marble,
an unseen finish line lies hidden in the clouds.

Please remember: irony and pain;
the pain had lived long inside his heart
and kept on growing—as though
each elegy he wrote adored him
obsessively and wanted
him alone to be its hero—

but ladies and gentlemen—your patience,
please, we're nearly through—I don't know
quite how to put it; something like tenderness,
the almost timid smile,
the momentary doubt, the hesitation,
the tiny pause in flawless arguments.

SELF-PORTRAIT, NOT WITHOUT DOUBTS

Enthusiasm moves you in the morning,
by evening you lack the nerve
even to glance at the blackened page.
Always too much or too little,
just like those writers
who sometimes bother you:
some so modest, minimal,
and underread,
that you want to call out—
hey, friends, courage,
life is beautiful,
the world is rich and full of history.
Others, proud and serious, are distinguished
by their erudition
—gentlemen, you too must die someday,
you say (in thought).
The territory of truth
is plainly small,
narrow as a path above a cliff.
Can you stick
to it?
Perhaps you've strayed already.
Do you hear laughter

or apocalyptic trumpets?
Perhaps both,
a dissonance, ungodly grating—
a knife that skates
along the glass and whistles gladly.

CONVERSATION

A chat with friends, sometimes
about nothing, TV or the movies,
or more important conversations, earnest talk
on torture, suffering, and hunger,
but also on easy amorous adventures,
"she said this, so he thought that."

Perhaps we talk too much,
like the French tourists I overheard
on a Greek mountain's steep slope,
careless in the Delphic labyrinth
(caustic comments on the hotel dinner).
We don't, we can't know,

if we'll be saved,
if our microscopic souls,
which have committed no evil
and likewise done no good,
will answer a question posed in an unknown tongue.
Will poetry's epiphany suffice,

delight in the staccato of past music,
the sight of a river and air entering
August's warm towers,
and longing for the sea, always fresh, new.

Or moments of celebration and the sense
they bring, that something has suddenly

returned and we can't live without it (but we can),
do they outweigh the years of emptiness and anger,
months of forgetfulness, impatience —
we don't know, we can't know,
if we'll be saved
when time ends.

OLD MARX

He can't think.
London is damp,
in every room someone coughs.
He never did like winter.
He rewrites past manuscripts
time and again, without passion.
The yellow paper
is fragile as consumption.

Why does life race
stubbornly toward destruction?
But spring returns in dreams,
with snow that doesn't speak
in any known tongue.
And where does love fit
within his system?
Where you find blue flowers.

He despises anarchists,
idealists bore him.
He receives reports from Russia,
far too detailed.
The French grow rich.
Poland is common and quiet.
America never stops growing.
Blood is everywhere,

perhaps the wallpaper needs changing.
He begins to suspect
that poor humankind
will always trudge
across the old earth
like the local lunatic
shaking her fists
at an unseen God.

TO THE SHADE OF ALEKSANDER WAT

Newly arrived at infinity—which turned out to resemble an elongated, vastly improved Wolomin Street—he received, upon entering, a gift in the shape of Schumann's music, bursting with rapture and chaos (the first movement of the first sonata for violin and piano as performed by two insufferable, but, we must concede, very gifted cherubim).

Later a certain learned rabbi parsed the distinctions between a silken and a stony death, and the famed theologian P. gave a lengthy lecture on "The Old, New, and Even Newer Testaments in Wat's Postwar Opus."

"Pain as a Pivotal Experience" and "An Inborn Gift for Synthesizing Unlike Objects" were the topics of other talks, which were received less attentively since afterward eternity was scheduled to perform and an orchestra of swarthy gypsies in snug tuxes played without pausing, without end.

NIGHT IS A CISTERN

Night is a cistern. Owls sing. Refugees tread meadow roads
with the loud rustling of endless grief.
Who are you, walking in this worried crowd.
And who will you become, who will you be
when day returns, and ordinary greetings circle round.

Night is a cistern. The last pairs dance at a country ball.
High waves cry from the sea, the wind rocks pines.
An unknown hand draws the dawn's first stroke.
Lamps fade, a motor chokes.
Before us, life's path, and instants of astronomy.

STORM

The storm had golden hair flecked with black
and moaned in a monotone, like a simple woman
giving birth to a future soldier, or a tyrant.

Vast clouds, multistoried ships
surrounded us, and lightning's scarlet strands
scattered nervously.

The highway became the Red Sea.
We moved through the storm like a sheer valley.
You drove; I watched you with love.

EVENING, STARY SACZ

The sun sets behind the market square, and nettles reflect
the small town's imperfections. Teapots whistle in the houses,
like many trains departing simultaneously.
Bonfires flame on meadows and their long sighs
weave above the trees like drifting kites.
The last pilgrims return from church uncertainly.
TV sets awaken, and instantly know all,
like the demons of Alexandria with swindlers' swarthy faces.
Knives descend on bread, on sausage, on wood, on offerings.
The sky grows darker; angels used to hide there,
but now it's just a police sergeant on his departed motorcycle.
Rain falls, the cobbled streets grow black.
Little abysses open between the stones.

BLAKE

I watch William Blake, who spotted angels
every day in treetops
and met God on the staircase
of his little house and found light in grimy alleys—

Blake, who died
singing gleefully
in a London thronged
with streetwalkers, admirals, and miracles,

William Blake, engraver, who labored
and lived in poverty, but not despair,
who received burning signs
from the sea and from the starry sky,

who never lost hope, since hope
was always born anew like breath,
I see those who walked like him on graying streets,
headed toward the dawn's rosy orchid.

NOTES FROM A TRIP TO FAMOUS EXCAVATIONS

You suddenly surface in a city that no longer is.
You turn up abruptly in a vast city
that isn't really there.
Three scrawny cats meow.
You notice campaign slogans on the walls
and know that the elections ended long ago,
emptiness was victorious and reigns
alongside a lazy sun.

Tourists wander nonexistent streets,
like Church Fathers—afflicted, alas,
by deepest acedia.
Bathhouse walls are bone-dry.
The kitchen holds no herbs,
the bedroom is sleepless.
We enter homes, gardens,
but no one greets us.

It seems we're stranded in a desert,
faced by the dry cruelty of sand
—just as in other places
that don't exist,
the native city
you never knew, will never know.
Even the death camps are lifeless.
Some friends are gone.

Past days have vanished,
they've hidden under Turkish tents,
in stasis, in a museum that's not there.
But just when everything is gone
and only lips move timidly
like a young monk's mouth,
a wind stirs, a sea wind,
bearing the promise of freshness.

A gate in the wall leans open,
and you glimpse life stronger than oblivion;
at first you don't believe your eyes—
gardeners kneel, patiently
tending the dark earth while laughing servants
cart great piles of fragrant apples.
The wooden wagons rattle on thick stones,
water courses through a narrow trough,

wine returns to the pitchers,
and love comes back to the homesteads
where it once dwelled,
and silently regains its absolute
kingly power
over the earth and over me.
Look, a flame stirs from the ashes.
Yes, I recognize the face.

ZURBARÁN

Zurbarán painted by turns
Spanish saints
and still lifes,
and thus the objects
lying on heavy tables
in his still lifes
are likewise holy.

NOTO

TO GEORGIA AND MICHAEL

Noto, a town that would be flawless
if only our faith were greater.

Noto, a baroque town where even
the stables and arbors are ornate.

The cathedral's cupola has collapsed, alas,
and heavy cranes surround it

like doctors in a hospital
tending the dangerously ill.

Afternoons town teenagers
gather on the main street

and bored stiff, whistle
like captive thrushes.

The town is too perfect
for its inhabitants.

III

TRAVELING BY TRAIN ALONG THE HUDSON

TO BOGDANA CARPENTER

River gleaming in the sun—

river, how can you endure the sight:
low crumpled train cars
made of steel, and in their small windows
dull faces, lifeless eyes.

Shining river, rise up.

How can you bear the orange peels,
the Coca-Cola cans, patches
of dirty snow that
once was pure.

Rise up, river.

And I too drowse in semidarkness
above a library book
with someone's pencil marks,
only half living.

Rise up, lovely river.

THE GREEKS

I would have liked to live among the Greeks,
talk with Sophocles' disciples,
learn the rites of secret mysteries,

but when I was born the pockmarked
Georgian still lived and reigned,
with his grim henchmen and theories.

Those were years of memory and grief,
of sober talks and silence;
there was little joy—

although a few birds didn't know this,
a few children and trees.
To wit, the apple tree on our street

blithely opened its white blooms
each April and burst
into ecstatic laughter.

GREAT SHIPS

This is a poem about the great ships that wandered the oceans
And groaned sometimes in deep voices, grumbling about fog and
    submerged peaks,
But usually they sliced the pages of tropical seas in silence,
Divided by height, category, and class, just like our societies and hotels.
Down below poor emigrants played cards, and no one won
While on the top deck Claudel gazed at Ysé and her hair glowed.

And toasts were raised to a safe trip, to coming times,
Toasts were raised, Alsatian wine and champagne from France's finest
    vineyards,
Some days were static, windless, when only the light seeped steadily,
Days when nothing happened but the horizon, which traveled with
    the ship,
Days of emptiness and boredom, playing solitaire, repeating the
    latest news,
Who'd been seen with whom in a tropical night's shade, embracing
    beneath a peach-colored moon.

But filthy stokers tirelessly tossed coal into open flaming mouths
And everything that is now already existed then, though in condensed
    form.
Our days already existed and our hearts baked in the blazing stove,
And the moment when I met you may also have existed, and my mistrust

Brittle as a faience plate, and my faith, no less frail and capricious,
And my searches for the final answer, my disappointments and discoveries.

Great ships: some sunk suddenly, arousing consciences and fear,
Gaining deathless fame, becoming stars of special bulletins.
Others went peacefully, waned without a word in provincial ports,
    in dockyards,
Beneath a coat of rust, a ruddy fur of rust, a slipcover of rust, and waited
For the final transformation, the last judgment of souls and objects,
They still wait patiently, like chess players in Luxembourg Garden nudging
    pieces a fraction of an inch or so.

ERINNA OF TELOS

She was nineteen when she died.
We don't know if she was lovely and flirtatious,
or if perhaps she looked like those
intelligent, dry girls in glasses
from whom mirrors are kept hidden.
She left behind just a few hexameters.
We suspect that she strove
with the secret, uncertain ambition of introverts.
Her parents loved her to distraction.
We speculate that she wanted to express
some vast truth about life, ruthless
on the surface, sweet within,
about August nights, when the sea
breathes and shines and sings like a starling,
and about love, ineffable and precious.
We don't know if she cried when she met darkness.
She left only a few hexameters
and an epigram about a cricket.

OF KINGDOMS

I LIKE TO DREAM OF THOSE
DEAD KINGDOMS —SU TUNG-P'O

I like to dream of those kingdoms
where brass glitters and sings,
and fires flame upward on the hilltops,
and someone's love dwells in them.
Later afternoon, in November,
I travel by commuter train
after a long walk;
around me are tired office workers
and a mournful old lady
clutching a dachshund.
The conductor, alas,
makes an awkward shaman.
Life strides over us like Gulliver,
loudly laughing and crying.

SYRACUSE

City with the loveliest name, Syracuse;
don't let me forget the dim
antiquity of your side streets, the pouting balconies
that once caged Spanish ladies,
the way the sea breaks on Ortygia's walls.

Plato met defeat here, escaped with his life,
what can be said about us, unreal tourists.
Your cathedral rose atop a Greek temple
and still grows, but very slowly,
like the heavy pleas of beggars and widows.

At midnight fishing boats radiate
sharp light, demanding prayers
for the perished, the lonely, for you,
city abandoned on a continent's rim,
and for us, imprisoned in our travels.

SUBMERGED CITY

That city will be no more, no halos
of spring mornings when green hills
tremble in the mist and rise
like barrage balloons —

and May won't cross its streets
with shrieking birds and summer's promises.
No breathless spells,
no chilly ecstasies of springwater.

Church towers rest on the ocean's floor,
and flawless views of leafy avenues
fix no one's eyes.

And still we live on calmly,
humbly — from suitcases,
in waiting rooms, on airplanes, trains,

and still, stubbornly, blindly, we seek an image,
the final form of things
between inexplicable fits
of mute despair —

as if vaguely remembering
something that cannot be recalled,
as if that submerged city were traveling with us,
always asking questions,

and always unhappy with our answers—
exacting, and perfect in its way.

EPITHALAMIUM

FOR ISCA AND SEBASTIAN

Without silence there would be no music.
Life paired is doubtless more difficult
than solitary existence—
just as a boat on the open sea
with outstretched sails is trickier to steer
than the same boat drowsing at a dock, but schooners
after all are meant for wind and motion,
not idleness and impassive quiet.

A conversation continued through the years includes
hours of anxiety, anger, even hatred,
but also compassion, deep feeling.
Only in marriage do love and time,
eternal enemies, join forces.
Only love and time, when reconciled,
permit us to see other beings
in their enigmatic, complex essence,
unfolding slowly and certainly, like a new settlement
in a valley or among green hills.

It begins from one day only, from joy
and pledges, from the holy day of meeting,
which is like a moist grain;

then come the years of trial and labor,
sometimes despair, fierce revelation,
happiness and finally a great tree
with rich greenery grows over us,
casting its vast shadow. Cares vanish in it.

GATE

TO BARBARA TORUŃCZYK

Do you love words as a shy magician loves the moment of quiet
after he's left the stage, alone in a dressing room where
a yellow candle burns with its greasy, pitch-black flame?

What yearning will encourage you to push the heavy gate, to sense
once more the odor of that wood and the rusty taste of water from an
    ancient well,
to see again the tall pear tree, the proud matron who presented us
aristocratically with its perfectly formed fruit each fall,
and then fell into mute anticipation of the winter's ills?

Next door a factory's stolid chimney smoked and the ugly town kept still,
but the indefatigable earth worked on beneath the bricks in gardens,
our black memory and the vast pantry of the dead, the good earth.

What courage does it take to budge the heavy gate,
what courage to catch sight of us again,
gathered in the little room beneath a Gothic lamp—
mother skims the paper, moths bump the windowpanes,
nothing happens, nothing, only evening, prayer; we wait . . .

We lived only once.

NEW YEAR'S EVE, 2004

You're at home listening
to recordings of Billie Holiday,
who sings on, melancholy, drowsy.
You count the hours still
keeping you from midnight.
Why do the dead sing peacefully
while the living can't free themselves from fear?

NO CHILDHOOD

And what was your childhood like? a weary
reporter asks near the end.
There was no childhood, only black crows
and tramcars starved for electricity,
fat priests in heavy chasubles,
teachers with faces of bronze.
There was no childhood, just anticipation.
At night the maple leaves shone like phosphorus,
rain moistened the lips of dark singers.

MUSIC HEARD

Music heard with you
was more than music
and the blood that flowed through our arteries
was more than blood
and the joy we felt
was genuine
and if there is anyone to thank,
I thank him now,
before it grows too late
and too quiet.

BALANCE

I watched the arctic landscape from above
and thought of nothing, lovely nothing.
I observed white canopies of clouds, vast
expanses where no wolf tracks could be found.

I thought about you and about the emptiness
that can promise one thing only: plenitude—
and that a certain sort of snowy wasteland
bursts from a surfeit of happiness.

As we drew closer to our landing,
the vulnerable earth emerged among the clouds,
comic gardens forgotten by their owners,
pale grass plagued by winter and the wind.

I put my book down and for an instant felt
a perfect balance between waking and dreams.
But when the plane touched concrete, then
assiduously circled in the airport's labyrinth,

I once again knew nothing. The darkness
of daily wanderings resumed, the day's sweet darkness,
the darkness of the voice that counts and measures,
remembers and forgets.

MORNING

Sunday morning, the wind has washed our minds,
the streets are bleak as a monastic regimen.
The young still sleep in their white tents,
and only the elderly head churchwards.
A ginkgo, still clinging to its leaves,
aglow with autumn's yellow fire,
announces that the moment has arrived.
Sunday morning, above the roofs of palaces and houses,
somber chimes hold conversations
while little bells laugh; Dominicans
and Norbertines exchanging telegrams.
Clad in bronze, the Planty Garden monuments
doubtless long for normal skin,
for flesh and aching heads, but eternity has its demands.

We quarreled here once, do you remember,
I looked for you in evening's labyrinth;
I held a book, you wore a summer dress
(the book went unread, but the dress spread
like the jacket of a Neoplatonic tract).
A bronze Boy-Zelenski gazed at me, his eyes
retained the image of a firing squad,
that masterpiece of Prussian architecture.
The wind washed minds and streets, it washed the sun.
Georg Trakl died a few hundred yards away,

killed by ecstasy or despair.
And we sat on that bench late one night
and tried to hear the ocean.
The moon was full, the stars ran quietly.

The moment came, after long negotiations,
broken off and taken up, abandoned once again,
when the past, wise and dry as parchments,
decided to make peace with petty day,
with the morning's improvisation, its damp breath,
my thoughts' dampness, my unrest,
and a delegation of the dead—poets, but also night watchmen,
experienced students of the darkness, and midwives,
who knew how bodies opened—
agreed that it was high time,
in silence, Sunday morning, when trees
flame peacefully, agreed conditionally
that I should wake and realize that the moment had arrived,
the moment had arrived—and would be gone.

OLD MARX (2)

I try to envision his last winter,
London, cold and damp, the snow's curt kisses
on empty streets, the Thames's black water,
chilled prostitutes lit bonfires in the park.
Vast locomotives sobbed somewhere in the night.
The workers spoke so quickly in the pub
that he couldn't catch a single word.
Perhaps Europe was richer and at peace,
but the Belgians still tormented the Congo.
And Russia? Its tyranny? Siberia?

He spent evenings staring at the shutters.
He couldn't concentrate, rewrote old work,
reread young Marx for days on end,
and secretly admired that ambitious author.
He still had faith in his fantastic vision,
but in moments of doubt
he worried that he'd given the world
just a new version of despair;
then he'd close his eyes and see nothing
but the scarlet darkness of his lids.

DOLPHINS

The sun sets and prying pelicans fly just above the sea's smooth skin;
you watch a fisherman killing a caught fish, invincibly convinced of
     his humanity,
while rosy clouds commence their slow, solemn march to the night's
     foothills—
you stay a moment, waiting to see dolphins
—maybe they'll dance their famous, friendly tango once again—
here, on the Gulf of Mexico, where you find tire marks and mussels
     along the broad beaches,
and energetic crabs that exit the sand like workers deserting a
     subterranean factory en masse.
You notice abandoned, rusty loading towers.
You walk along a stone lock and wave to a few anglers,
modest types, fishing not for sport, just in hope
of postponing the last supper.
A vast, brick-red ship from Monrovia sails up the port canal
like some bizarre imaginary beast boasting of its own oddness,
and briefly blocks the horizon.
You think: it's worth seeking the backwaters, provincial spots
that remember much, but are uncommonly discreet,
quiet, humble places, rich, though, in caches, hidden pockets of
     memory like hunters' jackets in the fall,
the bustling town's outskirts, wastelands where nothing happens,
     there are no famous actors,
politicians and journalists don't appear,

but sometimes poetry is born in emptiness,
and you start to think that your childhood halted here,
here, far from long-familiar streets —
since absence after all can't calculate distance in light-years or kilometers,
instead it calmly waits for your return, doubtless wondering what's
become of you. It meets you without fanfare and says:
Don't you know me? I'm a stamp from your vanished collection,
I'm the stamp that showed you
your first dolphin on a backdrop of unreal, misty blue. I'm the sign
of travel.
Unmoving.

ORGAN TUNING

Someone was tuning the organ in an empty church.
In a Gothic hall a waterfall boomed.
The voices of the tortured and schoolchildren's laughter
mixed with my vertical breath.

In an empty church someone tuned the organ
and tinkered with the pipes' wild anarchy,
demolished houses, flung thunderbolts, then built
a city, airport, highway, stadium.

If only I could see the organist!
Catch sight of his face, his eyes!
If I could trace the movements of his hands,
I might understand where he's taking us,
us and those for whom we care,
children, animals, shadows.

FIREMEN'S HELMETS

I scrutinize firemen's helmets
which reflect clouds
and a microscopic glider.
The fire will start up soon,
in an hour or so.

Beauty and fear are always paired—
like the time I learned
Marek had died and wandered
through a cold Paris, from which
summer was slowly departing.

A BIRD SINGS IN THE EVENING

TO LILLIE ROBERTSON

Above the vast city, plunged in darkness,
breathing slowly, as if its earth were scorched,
you, who sang once for Homer
and for Cromwell, maybe even
over Joan of Arc's gray ashes,
you raise your sweet lament again,
your bright keening; no one hears you,
only in the lilac's black leaves, where
unseen artists hide,
a nightingale stirred, a little envious.
No one hears you, the city is in mourning
for its splendid days, days of greatness,
when it too could grieve
in an almost human voice.

WAIT FOR AN AUTUMN DAY

(FROM EKELÖF)

Wait for an autumn day, for a slightly
weary sun, for dusty air,
a pale day's weather.

Wait for the maple's rough, brown leaves,
etched like an old man's hands,
for chestnuts and acorns,

for an evening when you sit in the garden
with a notebook and the bonfire's smoke contains
the heady taste of ungettable wisdom.

Wait for afternoons shorter than an athlete's breath,
for a truce among the clouds,
for the silence of trees,

for the moment when you reach absolute peace
and accept the thought that what you've lost
is gone for good.

Wait for the moment when you might not
even miss those you loved
who are no more.

Wait for a bright, high day,
for an hour without doubt or pain.
Wait for an autumn day.

KATHLEEN FERRIER

(1912–1953)

TO ANNA MARIA AND KAROL BERGER

It's just a voice.
It's just a voice, and we don't know
if it still belongs to a body,
or to the air alone.

The voice of a girl journeying
to Carlisle in a used Morris.

Just think, how many different voices
sounded in her life's brief span.
Goebbels's hysterical cry.
The moaning of the wounded, prisoners' whispers.

Declamations in school auditoriums
(epics praising the tyrant).
So many lies in our throats.

She died of cancer,
not from hunger like Simone Weil,
not in a camp like Mandelstam.

She never studied in a conservatory
and yet the purest music
speaks through her.

She liked the songs of Schubert and Mahler,
Bruno Walter counseled her.

A girl's voice,
innocent, sings Handel's arias.

Listening, you think
here was a chance
for a better human race,

but the record ends
and you return to your usual mistrust—

as if the song promised too much,
more than silence or exhaustion.

LIFE IS NOT A DREAM

In the beginning, freezing nights and hatred.
Red Army soldiers fired automatic pistols
at the sky, trying to strike the Highest Being.
Mother cried, perhaps remembering
the sentimental stories of her childhood.
Coldwater Street ran beside the river
as if trying to outrace it—
or to reach its distant sources,
still pure beyond a doubt,
recalling the dawn's joy.

If life is a dream,
then the phoenix may actually exist.
But in Krakow life revived
under the sign of common pigeons:
in the Planty Gardens, alongside veterans
clad in the tattered uniforms
of at least three armies,
young beauties made appearances,
and music-loving plane trees donned
their finest new foliage outside Symphony Hall.

Should one honor local gods?
A beggar at the marketplace in Lucca
moved from stand to stand
garnering tributes—proud as Diana.

It's more difficult to find nymphs
where we live, though,
and great Pan didn't leave his calling card.
Important memories—stern monuments
to monotheism—were inscribed
only in the trees and on church walls.

We tried courage, since there was no exit.
We tried cunning, but it failed.
We tried patience and fell asleep.
We wrote poems like leaflets and leaflets
like pages from burgeoning epics.
Dreams grew like hibiscus flowers.
Dark wells opened in the night.
We tried cynicism; some of us succeeded.
There was great joy, don't forget.
We tried time; it was tasteless, like water.

Finally, much later, for unknown
reasons, the clocks began
to revolve ever faster above us,
as in archival, silent films.
And life went on, inevitable life,
so skeptical, so practiced,
coming back to us so insistently
that one day we felt the taste of ordinary failure,
of common tragedy upon our lips,
which was a kind of triumph.

IT DEPENDS

YOU MUST BE SOMEWHERE, RIGHT? —NICK FLYNN

Birds (sandpipers) hop on the beach at Galveston.
"La plupart des hommes meurent de chagrin"—says Buffon
(as quoted in Volume One of Claudel's diaries).
R. thinks American poets are unintelligent.
—Yet nobleness exists, if only in a painting:
Christ's face in the Caravaggio at S. Luigi dei Francesi
(I couldn't tear myself away, I couldn't go).
It depends who, I answer: I defend American poets.
Summer, endless dusk, and then the stars like lanterns.
We discuss the emptiness of recent French poetry.
But "rien" is such a lovely word! Better than nothing.
Even the ocean seems happy at noon.
Forests burn: resin has its brief moment of bliss.
We eat ice cream on the café terrace. The speakers are playing "Yesterday."
Notes from a civil war: truce or armistice?
Suddenly I move to Aix-en-Provence, I don't know how.
Evening crowds on the streets, anticipation.
I push through a dense thicket of onlookers and ask:
What's happening? God's coming back. But it's just a dream.

AMERICA'S SUN

(FROM EICHENDORFF, FROM KRYNICKI)

Outside the window, America's blinding sun.
In a dark room, at a table
sits a man, no longer young,
who thinks about what he's lost
and what remains.

I am that man.
I try to guess what losses
the future holds.
I still don't know what I'll discover.

ANTENNAS IN THE RAIN

I saw the sea and oranges.

First snow—ladies and gentlemen, a moment's silence please.

Breaking news: Bach woke again and sings.

Time kept its word (it always does).

Reading Milosz by an open window. The swallows' sudden trill.

Chapels beneath the linden trees in summer; bees pray.

"Carpe diem." He seized the day, but when he checked his prey that

evening, he found night.

—You really like libraries that much?

Carrots, onions, celery, prunes, almonds, powdered sugar, four large

apples, green are best (your love letter).

Don't get carried away. To say that Orthodox liturgies lack humor!

The hospital—pale invalids in gowns beside a tanned, smiling surgeon.

Why do you always write about cities?

If only we read poetry as carefully as menus in expensive restaurants . . .

"Periagoge"—Plato's notion of internal transformation.

The bulging Place de la Bastille—perhaps another Bastille is hiding

underneath.

Peonies like peasant girls in church.

"How can I miss you when you won't go away?" (country song).

Varieties of longing; the professor counted six.

Sign on a bus: AIR-CONDITIONED. Day trips—Wieliczka, Auschwitz.

The homeless clinging to radiators at a railroad station in December.

Vermeer's painting with a woman sitting safely on the stoop and

knitting: behind her a dark interior, in front, the street and light.

Irreconcilable.

The sun hurts, says the boy in the park.

B., reproachfully: I lived there, you know, and I'd never say there was

too much of Lvov!

Everything returns. Inspiration wanes and returns. Desire.

Comedy and tragedy; Simone Weil sees only tragedy.

Red poppies and black snow.

The smile of a woman, no longer young, reading on the train to Warsaw.

Oh, so you're the specialist in high style?

Delphi, full of tourists, open to mysteries.

The sea was angry at midnight: furious, to be frank.

And the Holocaust Museum in Washington—my childhood, my wagons,

my rust.

May evening: antennas in the rain.

Down Kanonicza Street screaming you sonofabitch.

Dolphins near Freeport: their favorite, ancient motion, like the symbol

scholars use for iambs.

A theater too tiny to hold Bergman's film.

Escape from one prison to the next.

After the announcement "zurückbleiben" at a subway stop in Berlin, a

quiet moment—the sound of absence.

Swifts in Krakow, stirred by summer, whistle loudly.

A weary verb goes back to the dictionary at night.

Mama always peeked at the novel's last page—to see what happened . . .

Truth is Catholic, the search for truth is Protestant (W. H. Auden).

Some experts predict that by the twenty-first century's end people will

no longer die.

Open up.

Pay the phone and gas, return the books, write Clare.

In the plane after dinner two pudgy theologians compare their pensions.

In Gliwice, Victory Street might have led to heaven but stops short, alas.

Will the escalator ever go where it takes us?

From a rushing train we saw fields and meadows—from the forest,

as from dreams, deer emerged.

Marble doesn't talk to clay (to time).

The salesgirl in a shoe store on the rue du Commerce, Vietnamese,

she tells you kneeling, I come from boat people.

I switched on the shortwave radio: someone sobbing in Bolivia.

Christ's face in S. Luigi dei Francesi.

One thing is sure: the world is alive and burns.

He read Hölderlin in a dingy waiting room.

Boat people—the only nation free of nationalism.

The spring rain's indescribable freshness.

Sliced with a knife.

"There are gods here too."

Fruit bursts.

I ask my father: "What do you do all day?" "I remember."

Delivery cars on a Greek highway, trademark Metafora.

On the sea's gleaming surface, a kayak, almost motionless—a compass

needle.

Remember the splendid cellist in a clown's lounge coat?

At night the lights of a vast refinery—a city where nobody lives.

Why do these moments end so quickly? Don't talk that way, speak

from within the moments.

Love for ordinary objects, unrequited.

Rowers on a green river, chasing time.

Poetry is joy hiding despair. But under the despair—more joy.

Speak from within.

It's not about poetry.

Don't speak, listen.

Don't listen.

Printed in the USA
CPSIA information can be obtained
at www.ICGtesting.com
LVHW091146150724
785511LV00005B/572